A Celebration
of Poets
Showcase Edition

Printing and Binding by The Maple-Vail Manufacturing Group

Poetry has been the reflection of humanity since time began. James Russell Lowell once defined poetry as "something to make us better and wiser by continually revealing those types of beauty and truth which God has set in all men's souls." Poets find the wisdom within their souls to act with grace as they record the events which transform their lives, and by their writing, give all of us the gift of inspiration.

How many of us have shared the joy of a child's birth with a card containing a few lines of verse, or wept with a grieving family as a poem is read at the funeral? Who has not sung the poetic words of a favorite song, or tried to write a poem expressing the first fruits of love? As we experience poetry in its highest forms, we realize that others have felt the emotions and urges that we feel, and with the knowledge that we are not alone in our feelings, we gain confidence and poise to meet our challenges head on.

What makes poetry so universal is that anyone, anywhere can be a poet. You do not have to be a scholar to enjoy and receive the vitality of poetry. A poet simply strives to capture in words the essence of the human condition as he or she experiences it–the tangible form of pure spirit. A young child full of bright-eyed wonder can write as moving a poem on what it means to be alive as her grandmother who reminisces about days gone by. The business man and student alike can understand the feelings expressed by a farmer who witnesses and records the transpiring awe of watching his crops grow through the wet spring earth. Poetry knows only the boundaries of the human soul.

While the ancient Greeks felt that one could not write poetry without consulting the Muse, a moment to look inside one's self, and patience in recording the vision, is all that is really needed to write poetry. Of course, what keeps most of us from writing a moving poem is the effort it takes to craft words so that the emotions are expressed as we feel them. Some lucky poets find the exact words the first time, but most poets labor intensely to create a gift that others can find meaningful. Thankfully, reading and enjoying poetry takes less effort.

While poetry is universal in its ability to transcend time and place, part of its lure to us as individuals lies in its varied "music"–the rhythm each poem has when read. When a poem is written, a rhythm develops which lends beauty and augments meaning. Think of a poem you've heard at a wedding. Most sound light and airy in celebration of the beauty of love. In contrast, a poem commemorating the passing of a hero often is somber and moves slowly and meditatively as it is read. The writer creates a poem by manipulating words just as a musician uses musical notes to create not only the right meaning, but the right sound to fully convey the emotion.

The poems which follow are the distilled essence of life. Whether life shattering or peaceful, these impressions and visions will inspire you in your journey through this world. As you read the carefully crafted words, you may smile as you revisit a great moment which exists only in your memory, or you may find a tear reluctantly seeking an outlet as a sentimental feeling is expressed. In either event, think of your unguarded response as a "thank you" to the men and women, young and old, who have shared with you their vision of humanity.

The poet's eye, in a fine frenzy rolling,
Doth glance from heaven to earth, from earth to heaven,
And as imagination bodies forth
The forms of things unknown, the poet's pen
Turns them into shape and gives to airy nothing
A local habitation and a name.
—William Shakespeare, *A Midsummer Night's Dream*
Act V, Scene 1

CRITICALLY POISED

by Marc Giroux

Critically Poised
Synaptic
The blade edge rush the brightly lit desires
of your life go past
Burdened in step with the weight of choice
Arm in arm with expectations,
obligations, benefactions.

Critically Poised
Hesitant
The shriek of decision
The sacrifice of wants
to work with a net
Or celebrate the risk and reach uncompromising
to find that once courageous step,
moving, deciding

Critically Poised
Relentless the inconsiderate balance
The search for quiet
before it goes by to settle in and see - Just. See.
To focus on your pursuit and in the throbbing silence...step.

Ode to a Weed . . .

– William N. Brower, Jr.

A poet once wrote of the majestic tree,
while I choose as my subject the lowly weed.
Though it can be lovely when it flowers with a grace,
it is mostly noted for growing in the wrong place.

Its persistence must be noted and that is a fact,
for it will grow in concrete if there is a crack.

In flower beds they grow for free,
and always stand taller for the neighbors to see.

Yes, you can pull them all day and into the night,
but on the morrow they're back in sight.

In our vegetable gardens it's much the same,
for the tenacious weed is always our bane.

They spread their seeds on the wind with nary a care,
and where you don't want them, they're always there.

Yes, a tree is lovely, we've all agreed,
but I take my hat off to the lowly weed.

GRANDMA'S SHOE

- J. Sack

I saw a mouse in Grandma's shoe.
It was yesterday,
But when I tried to tell her,
She just smiled and walked away.
She motioned for me to follow
As she nestled in her chair,
And in the glow of firelight
We both just waited there.
As soon as we were quiet,
A shadow did appear.

I shuddered with excitement
As the shadow scurried near.
It held a piece of Grandma's cheese
in its tiny hands,
And when it finished eating it,
It washed its face and then
It scurried back across the floor,
Back to where it was before,
And in the dim light we could see
The mouse climb in her shoe.
No wonder Grandma only smiled,
She already knew.

FEEL THE COLOR
ALL AROUND

- Sondra L. Simmons

Feel the color all around
The blackness of souls,
Unleashed and unbound
The blackness is in
The rhythm of the walk
The beat of the ancient drums
Is heard in the talk

Feel the pulsating of pride
Too strong to ignore,
Too powerful to deny
Feel the color all around

The color of blackness,
Dark and strong
Revealing its mysteries
In rhythm and song
Listen to its laughter,
Shiver at its screams
Sense its eruptiveness
From injustice and denied dreams
Look at the blackness,
The glory unbound
The beauty of the rainbow
Feel the color all around

FISHING
- Tina Brunner

Sitting here in paradise,
Thinking life is pretty nice.

Underneath the swaying trees,
Bobber bobbing in the breeze.

You kick back and take in the view,
All of the sudden one hit, then two!

He grabs a hold of the bait,
You no longer need to wait.

It's like a rush, an inner flight,
It's the thrill of the fight.

If inner peace is what you're wishing,
There is nothing like plain old fishing.

SEAMSTRESS
- Jennifer J. Elliott

I'm sewing my anger inside.
I'm quilting my sorrows down.
My frustrations are tucked
So an appliqued smile shows,
But when the seams rip,
I'll explode!

ONLY HUMAN
- Tara Kerstetter

You read it in the papers
This fight is nothing new
But I don't understand it
I haven't got a clue

Too blinded by the ignorance
To really see the light
And to know it doesn't matter
If your skin is black or white

I hope that others feel this way
And decide to reach out
And show this world what getting along
Is really all about

I've made my big decision
I've found my destined place
It may be an old fashioned concept
But it's called the human race

MORNING
- Lynor Mortensen

In the morning glow
As it spreads over the land
Nature awakes from its sleep
And shakes the new day's hand

The Un-American Game

- Robert J. Brennecke, Sr.

The day was hot and humid, but coolness filled the night.
We came to see a Baseball game, instead we saw a fight.

The Little League was here this eve to see their heroes play.
They'd saved up all their pennies for this their special day.

The Catcher called for fastball, the Pitcher let it fly.
It went straight for the batter, the crowd let out a sigh.

The batter let the bat go, its flight was straight and true.
What happened next was not the game, that everybody knew.

The dugouts soon were empty, all players charging fast
To smash the other's body, alas the die was cast.

The Little Leaguers sat real still, their faces filled with fright.
It really wasn't Baseball that they were shown that night.

I ask you friend, is this the game that we have come to love,
To hit and kick and holler, to push and curse and shove?

If that's the case, I'll tell you now, I'll teach my kids with care
To find some other heroes who play hard and fast, but fair.

Ryan

- Debra K. Varner

Once a bug, a tree, a red bird, and a frog
began to argue about a young boy they knew.
The BUG said, "He's Just Like Me
sneaking into the cupboards when no one is watching."
The TREE said, "No, he's Just Like Me,
growing straight and tall.
He is up to my branches already,
quite tall for his 14 years."
The RED BIRD did not agree:
"Everyone just look and see his feelings are fragile,
Just Like Me, and our feathers match, can't you see."
The FROG, who was not to be outdone said,
"Not so, he's Just Like Me,
a prince in disguise. You will see,
hidden within his teenage life
is the man he will be."
Then an Eagle landed in the tree.
He cried out in a loud voice, and all listened to hear,
"He is like all of you, can't you see:
He is a bug,
a tree,
a red bird,
and a frog.
Let Everyone Look and See!"

August—5 P.M.

- Marjorie Millison

The sky drips its muggy heat unto the streets below.
I press through the rush hour maze,
feeling like a bird that's trapped—
trapped within walls—
beating itself against the panes.
I'm caged by corporate concrete and steel,
swept along by swarming crowds,
trapped masses, fragmented lives,
wearing expressionless faces with staring eyes.
Sweaty flesh converges,
crushing, rushing, closing in,
melting into the chaotic blur
of clang and clatter—blare and roar.
I breathe the thick, stifling heat.
The acrid stench of engine exhaust
sticks in my throat. My burning eyes watch
as a city struggles to cleanse itself,
and a people struggle to escape—
to be free, to fly away
to the coolness
to the silences
of open skies.

My wounded wings beat, beat against the panes—
and the pains of free flying spirits—trapped.

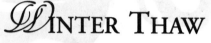INTER THAW

- Sharon Durell

The Wind held its Breath
. . . when the Sun came Out
And the Snow began to Glisten;

The Ice lost its Grip
. . . with a Crack! and a Shout!
And Snowmen came up Missin'.

EVERIE 1

- Vincent J. Biondo

The days go by, slowly it seems,
And recollections–
Reveries, if you please–
Keep crowding in,
Blurred by time and its
Accompanying forgetfulness–
Not total, but deceptively
Insidious, rendering each
Scenario as through
A fog: shifting and swirling,
With neither shape nor form,
Nor substance tangible,
As though painted by a tipsy sailor aboard
A storm-tossed ship, anchored yet plunging
In wild gyrations to free itself,
But with no hope of ever doing so.

SILHOUETTES
- Timothy A. Loftin

Evening gives us absolutes in silhouettes displayed,
so clearly drawn a feathered leaf becomes a crystal blade.
All we see is perfect dark or simple glowing light,
no trace of in-between to blur a long day's final sight:
as in a man's last backward look before descent of night.

THE SUNSET
- Alvina Otto

Threads of pure gold
Lined the sunset sky.
Bright rose fades
Into clouds on high.

Deepest blue gives way
To green, to yellow gold,
Vivid red to rose,
To blue-rich and bold.

Swiftly fade the colors
As the sun sinks westerly.
The Moon rises in the east,
Now each star winks easterly.

Another cycle has been completed,
Another day is done.
One more day fulfilled,
Another cycle begun.

LONG LAKE

- Patrick Brandimore, Jr.

Algae suspended about their face
as air bubbles rise to the surface.
Buckled up,
'cause it's the law.
Buckled in,
to secure her sin.
Momma stumbles up the shore,
conjuring up car-jack confabulations
to secure the relations
with her estranged lover.
Seems she didn't want to bother with
Tinker Toys
or hugs from her boys,
who only wanted a little love,
not a shove
into a lake.

SUNSET

- Dorothy M. Clarke

Shimmering fingers of red and gold
Streak across the azure sky;
The sun sets in her fiery orb,
While downy clouds float gently by;
Twilight serenely on earth descends
Stealing slowly from our sight;
Ever dimmer grows the day,
As evening drifts softly into night

GODS
- Annette Krizanich

black ants on the patio
diminutive pilgrims
at their bread-crumb shrine
dragged across the tile

deus ex machine I
pinched an ant
between thumb and forefinger
flicked it into the littered orb
of a patient yellow weaver

the hairy little god
at the center of fate
twisted the dancer in silk
sucked the spirit from its shell

breezes set the drained bodies fluttering
a hurricane of dead brown leaves
in a chapel doorway

MY SON JOHN
- Carol S. Johnson

The prettiest flower I ever had
was brought to me by a tiny lad,
for the smile on his lips when his
eyes met mine made an orchid out
of a dandelion.

$\mathcal{I}$ Am

- Kristine Kathryn Armbruster

I am big and full of painful wounds
I wonder what it would be like to lie on the sandy shore of the beach
I hear the waves calling to me, drawing me nearer and nearer to
their crashing sound against the rocks
I see an angel signaling for my presence on the shore
I want to be put out of my anguish and misery, but I must erase
these thoughts from my mind
I am big and full of painful wounds

I pretend to be free of pain
I feel no remorse upon myself, though I wish the pain would stop
I touch no solution with my mind
I worry about the well-being of my unborn
I cry when I think of the suffering being inflicted upon it
I am big and full of painful wounds

I understand not everyone has compassion for the mighty
creatures of the deep
I say to myself, "There is hope." When I am in doubt
I dream of being able to be free, frolicking with my "child" in
the depths of the ocean
I try to fight back the tears
I hope someday I will live life again for all it's worth
I am big and full of painful wounds

Why

- Elaine Barton

A lonely helmeted figure
In the dark on foreign sod,
Cold hard steel his security,
Guarding and communing with GOD.

From birth till age of draft,
We are taught "Thou shalt not kill."
Estranged transplants, now we're told
If you don't shoot first he will,

No chance to live out our life,
The many blessings infinite.
The breath of life for untimely death,
Seemingly the only thing in it,

The souls of many before us,
Courageous and confused as mine,
Have departed in the field of battle
Time after time after time.

Give my life for the safety of my son?
Likewise my dad had to die.
AND MY son will be bleeding too,
For security my blood won't buy.

So why do we serve the MASTER
Who we know in our hearts is greed?
Giving our bodies as fodder,
On which the war dragons feed.

Sugar Snow

- Marilyn Diamond

Last night while I lay sleeping,
Some gnomes or maybe elves
Stole into Mama's pantry
And took sugar from her shelves.

They sifted it through tree limbs,
Filled robin's empty nest.
They drifted it against the eaves
And scattered all the rest.

They piled it on fence posts,
They sprinkled it on cars.
It shines and gleams in ripples
Like a thousand gleaming stars.

Each pine bough's heavy laden,
And the clever little fellows
Have given every lamp post
A hat of white marshmallows.

And kitty seems to know it's sweet,
With each small step, she licks her feet.

Summer on My Street

- Leah G. Ordonez

the house up the street
sits on its haunches, waiting
for the others to make their move.

nothing ever moves, though,
because the air is thick
as molasses over a slow fire.

the air breathes slowly
down your neck, when the sun
isn't looking down your dress.

the very hours of the day
violate you with their
slow, inescapable hands.

no one dares walk out
on the street, not with
this many voyeurs.

For My Lois

- Kelly Campbell

If the sun were made of shadows,
and the stars were icy tears,
my Love for you would light the day
and warm the wintry years.

THE SUN AND THE VINE

- Nina Butcher

A shadow creeps unto the wall, capturing the sun's rays
The vine shivers in the cold, and for the light it prays
The vine reaches up to the sun, calling its name aloud
A shadow stands still, the shadow of a cloud
"Sun! Sun!" it cries, "Give me back the light!"
It withers with a sorrow and calmly comes the night
The clouds collide with others, their thunder chases wind
The vine looks up with hope, only rain the cloud did send
In the coming morning, dew set upon the leaves
The vine stands still, it cries and it grieves
The sun looks down upon it with love in his eyes
"Why do you cry, my vine, didn't you know that I would rise?"
The vine looks up with a dew as a tear
"My Sun, when you're away, I truly fear
Without your rays of joy
To the dark of night
And, oh, my Sun, I am terrified with fright."
The Sun replied, "My vine, do not fear, I raised you from a seed
I would never leave your side and will provide what you need
You may fear when I am gone, in every coming night
But, my precious vine, I tell you, you need the dark and rain
As much as you need the light."

Last Bouquet

- Holly Palmer

something sad about the leaving
from a home that sheltered you
kitchen walls that call for comfort
in plates of white and blue

something haunted in the garden
that grew with love and care
is calling out "remember me"
from redwood bench so bare

young trees bearing fruit at last
grapes grow tender vines
the cutting of the passion fruit
with honeysuckle twines

the pond lies melancholy low
bent willow weeping near
a meadowlark in nest close by
sings songs of yesteryear

a home was built on love that grew
as did the plains of green
a haven for a couple who
might realize their dream

the roses that were tendered through
grow heartily on their way
I arrest their tender blossom
and pick the last bouquet

Mantra in the Darkness

- Madonna N. Groom

The Spirit of Tesla
Borrowed by Marconi
Drifts along the midnight shadows

A mantra in the darkness . . .

The Taos hum?
A distant drum?
The Anasazi know

The mantra in the darkness . . .

Complexity fills new yearnings
With desire
To seek one's fortune

From the mantra in the darkness . . .

But how?
When, where?
The Chu'en Dynasty knows

About the mantra in the darkness . . .

For now you will have to
Close your eyes in the darkness
And join the mantra
To be one
With the one
That flows through you

Man's Dilemma

- Joan D. Rice

Choices,
Basis of sorrow.
Blaming Fate,
God,
Circumstance,
Man curses his self-created Hell.
In reality each one
Weaves his own web,
A trap,
At times with no escape.
And sometimes blindly,
With eyes open
But senses shut,
We evolve in an intricate labyrinth of
Winding passages,
The product of our own ignorance.
Lost in our prisons of darkness,
We stumble about for eons and eons,
Floating in our sea of confusion,
Drowning in our perpetual gloom,
Searching for the exit
Through which the light of truth
Will lead us to the
Path of Spiritual Freedom.

MOUNTAIN MAN RED
- Beth Rorrer

Mountain Man Red went down on a stormy night in May
The thunder boomed thru Delton Hollow
The lightning flashed and was gone
The moment Mountain Man Red went away

Most of his life he roamed the hills
The willows bent on his command
He stripped their bark and formed incredible art
From the Oak tress he carved beams
And built a structure fit for a king, Mountain Man Red

As a lad he could be found underneath that old loft
A pail in hand from stall to stall to milk Bessie and Blackie
He groomed the horses as they ate the food from the loft
Old Lead, the hunting dog, watched each twitch and
Collie lay under a shade tree
Little did they know what would happen to that old barn
As a result of Mountain Man Red

And did you ever hear echoes from the past
Or did they gather and roll together with a sound
Knowing it would be no more
The night that Mountain Man Red went down

A deserving honor, a status of valor
Tower over the hills of Delton Hollow
After all has been done and said
Don't tread on Mountain Man Red

Arachne's Circus
- Edwin L. Stephens

Under the silent tent of night,
the tireless strategist ventures,
throws endless filament.
Resolute, ruthless aerialist, Arachne,
artful spinner, performs a primordial
dance, symmetrically weaves
her intricate lace.
Casting, unreeling, connecting endless
angled spheres tensed by weed
and bush, she creates.

Posed high, eyes fixed upon the
web of her unique design, the catcher,
a heartless young vamp on a
dare-you-to rig awaits searchlight
dawn, her breakfast invitation
well concealed.

Fliers welcome;
no reservation required.

Autumn Maple
- Linda Potter

Undressing, she bares
Her arms to the biting cold,
Winter's passion play.

Moment
- Margaret Harvey

There is a haze upon the hills today
The washing moves idly with a light breeze's play.
The heat of the sun is yet to come,
And the bees in the blackberries gently hum.

The ripened wheat shimmers like a golden sea,
And a pigeon coos softly in the old apple tree.
There's a sweet smell of roses fresh with dew,
while butterflies dance in a colorful hue.

Then the drone of a tractor intrudes the mind,
Milk bottles clink, and as you turn you find
The sounds of the day are on the increase,
And gone is that precious quiet moment of peace.

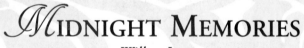idnight Memories
- Willow Jones

A diminishing sun holds the breaking dawn
in starlit routes
of ancient legends on forgotten moors.
Glazing mists shimmer fragments
in nocturnal eyes
to drift and bind with windswept leaves.
A silent rustle, an errant glow light softly
in memory's subtle embrace
sighing cool moisture and melodious strokes
in the silver tones of a moonlit song.

VOTE IN THE DARKNESS

- Patricia K. Chambers

Born in the inner city,
I've always been an outcast,
told by politicians that I was important,
but were they just wearing a mask?

I cast my vote in darkness,
and darkness is where I will stay
'cause I can't seem to plug into the system,
can't seem to wash it all away.

The suburbs have the say so
their money speaks loud and clear,
but they care little for the urban dwellers,
they can't see the poor child's tear.

But still I cast my vote in darkness,
hoping to end my blight,
hoping for truth and fairness,
a way to put an end to the night.

THE WATCHERS

- Nancy L. Gunning

As watchers of The Storm
they wait
knowing all too well
that men will falter
and will fail
beneath the horse that's pale.

And still they watch
the mindless march
the blind too dumb to see
nor will they stop
Time's vile assault
on immortality.

Good watchers pray
and still they wait
for knowledge that is True;
upon the path
that is self-made
the soul is born anew.

MUSICALE OF THE NIGHT

- Mary Senf

Musicale of the night
Gently depicting
The cascading notes
Permeate my being.
Now intonations of
Varied chords on a
Delightful flight
of studied cadence.

Sanguine Musicale
Seemingly float
And gesture in mounting notes,
Caressing the mind,
Beckoning the spirit
Awakening the heart.

Expectations of a secret note
In sacred bliss
A clandestine affair
With the Musicale of the Night.

Not a Sound She Made

- Lyn Paladino

On a dark road narrow and straight between
Dank fields under a silver sickle,
The buggy, black as grief, rode right lane edge.
Bright headlights speared the sultry summer night.
The on-coming pickup truck slowed, drew alongside
The buggy. A stone hurled. Motor revved.
A woman's outcry. Buggy wheels turned, turned.

The bearded man raised the lantern wick high
And placed the white lucky stone, hen's egg size,
On the table where the baby lay still.
He saw quiet on five faces holding
The half-circle of wavering light, five
Children honoring silence or his daze.
His wife reached, touched the baby's round cheek.

"Not a sound she made. Asleep in my arms,
She stretched twice, just kind of like when they dream."
He saw the rosette of blood in the baby's ear.
He placed his own to her heart. Nothing. None.
He thought of the living, waved them to bed
And sat vigil through lonely, tearless night,
Wishing the wolves leave to devour the wind.

The Lily Pond

- John Duckering

On bright summer days
When the wind blows forgetfully,
How quietly my heart sleeps,
So that then past becomes past
And time becomes a friend of mine,
Scenting my senses with roses and thyme.
Where the sweet apple trees and
Promising blossoms lie,
Scattered in petticoats of confetti cries.
Crazy Black Shellac Beetles scurry on
Spindly feet, dancing the crystal,
While the Lily Pond sleeps.
A troubled Scaly Brassy Dragon Fly
Dancing boldly upon her skin
Slides in rings and waltzing his merry tune,
Too soon, too soon,
Beneath a burning August Moon.
On bright summer nights,
When the moon cuts its way,
Quietly the clouds part and drift away.

Life's Five Senses
- Mary Elizabeth Thomas

I saw your sweet shyness all through the years,
That ever present smile I knew was sincere.
I basked in love you gave me so true.
So you see, my eyes beheld a miracle in you.

I heard your kind voice in a many different key.
The one I heard best was the key just for me.
The sound of your step as you entered the room
Made me hear sweet laughter and chased away gloom.

I still smell the fragrances that remind me of you,
Our strolls in the mornings, the air fresh with dew,
The sweat on your body after working all day,
Then the sweet, clean smell after bathing it away.

I touched you with love, and anger as well.
I touched you with warmth, never cold, you could tell.
I touched your lips and your eyes that were blind
To all the many faults that were especially mine.

I still taste the sweet pleasures we so eagerly spent.
The taste for a time was bitter, but now I must relent,
For you taught me lessons in living that are ever so true,
Quote, "Life is just what you make it, so it's all up to you."

You fill my soul's cellar with memories so rare.
May your earthly transition be just and fair,
For come some tomorrow we may meet someplace,
Two souls forever entwined in a lasting embrace.

The Proposal

- Cynthia Flexon

The candle flickers slowly
Their eyes sparkle in its light
There is magic in the air
On such an enchanted night

Quietly they speak in whispers
Even though they are all alone
Words of love should be spoken softly
With a sweet, melodic tone

He gives to her a single red rose
And pledges his devotion
She gives to him her heart's key
And mirrors his emotions

He takes her hand in his
And places a package on her palm
It's a box of soft, blue velvet
She struggles to remain calm

She opens the box slowly
As he caresses her cheek
A brilliant diamond shines from inside
And he begins to speak

"Say that you will be my wife
and I shall be truly blessed"
She throws her arms around him
And whispers "Yes. Yes. Yes."

THE MAN WHO DIED LAUGHING

- Michael S. Monroe

he laughed
for he knew life had no meaning
and people were stupid
and chickens laid eggs

he laughed at simplicity
at parties and carnivals
at frivolous people who had no direction

he laughed at the city
at trees
at parks
at the sun
at the moon
on the shores of heaven

it was all so hilarious
those dolts who knew nothing
the artists and singers
the players and lovers

he watched them dance
he watched their happiness
their ignorant bliss
their stormy loves

he laughed at them all
and they laughed right back
for he died without a smile

Songs of the Wind
- Michele Marie Hall

I'm a wild wind with nomadic names
of many tales that may vanish if not told.
From the beginning of time, I've played games
with dew-fresh grasses in the fields of gold.
I've traveled among mountains' purple peaks
to caress Heaven's soft serenity;
in the abyss of vast valleys and creeks
I have set the flaming fires of Hell free.
I wallow in the chirps of robins
and taste the sweet nectar from a white rose.
I am the wicked wrath of nature's sins,
churning the torrid twirls of tornadoes
and boughs and branches that sail in my ride.
I blow summer's fires to lofty heights
while weaning, weathered waters surf my tide.
I sing of soft melodious delights
upon an aria's bestial billows that grace
my bellowing haunted spirit that lives on.
Ageless, thus not even time can erase
my endless echoes, never to be gone.

Silent Lovesong
- Barbara Norman

On winter evenings
Lonely snowflakes tumble to
Arms of waiting pines.

United in Sorrow
- Angela Krizan

I've seen their tears and witnessed their pain.
Like groups of willows, standing bravely side by
side with heads bent, they join together to say goodbye.
From each other they draw the strength of oaks
to continue life without their friend.
Forming a row of guardian pines, each moving to
embrace those that join them, sharing their
sorrow and offering comfort to we who stand
in the shadows, helpless and saddened to see
those so young, without completely outstretched
branches, attempting to cope with the axes of choice.

Lonesome World
- Yvonne Young

Long ago before we were born,
The world was lonesome and bare.
The sky was blue, the clouds were white,
But there was just no one there.
So GOD made people, to live on the Earth,
To take care of the animals and trees.
But they took advantage of what they had,
And polluted the air and seas.
So here I sit staring far away,
Thinking of how it was then.
And now that I think of it, yes it's true,
The world is lonesome again.

THE FALL OF THE VERY FIRST SNOW

- Jeannie West

He was such a lonely man; his cell was cold and drear.
The winter sky shone through the bars and he knew his time was near.
The judge had said that he must die; what day he did not know,
But the guards would take him to his death
At the fall of the very first snow.

He was not afraid to die; his peace with GOD was made.
He owed his life for a wrong he'd done,
and he longed to get his debt paid!
The days just seemed to never end; time had never passed by so slow.
And he pleaded with GOD to take him
Before the fall of the very first snow.

Then a snow flake slowly drifted through his window overhead,
And silently it melted there on the sleeping convict's bed.
Then a guard came rushing into his cell and excitedly he cried,
"Wake up, convict, your time has come". . .
But the convict had already died.

Well, the news, it spread o'er the countryside and everybody asked, "Why?"
For the convict had robbed each one of them of the privilege
To watch him die. But not one of them could understand
What you and I both know, that the convict died a free man's death
At the fall of the very first snow.

Just a Man

- Thomas A. McClure

Now that I'm no longer here,
And now that I am gone,
Shall the memories be dear?
Shall all the words be fond?

When they gather all to sit
And chat of days gone by,
Will they think of me with wit,
Or with a saddened sigh?

Will my ills live after me?
Or will the good survive?
Did they know and did they see,
How hard I really tried?

So, my friends, just judge me true
Whenever you think of me;
I was just a man like you,
Not all that I should be.

OSTALGIA

- Laura L. Wright

Nostalgia, oh, how sweet to once again hear
her lovely name,
To find peace in seeing her here, and knowing
we still feel the same.
There is a whisper between her and I that will
always make me smile.
The whisper of memories shared, of how we walked
those many miles.
But still I know this journey will end, and our
ways will surely part.
And I'll remember again how it felt when first
she touched my heart.
I've seen her in the night and touched her in
my dreams,
But she'll never let me near to her, she wishes
only to be free.
Only somehow in my head I know her, and she'd
only do me harm.
And I remember how I held her when I fell victim
to her charm.
Still I lie in a motionless slumber, as she caresses
my weary head,
Knowing that I would see her again, as she held me in
this my hour of death.

Farmer's Prayer

- Debra H. Redd

Farming is an occupation, a trade.
It's one of the building blocks from which all our lives are made.

The farmer tills the soil and plants the seed
To produce the crops that provide food that we all need.

Farmers' prayers are never consistent, and vary from day to day,
He may pray for rain or sunshine, it's really hard to say.

From planting 'til harvest the time seems will never end,
But winter comes and the farmer can relax and prepare to begin again.

Farm families must work together, not apart.
To make farming successful, you have to love
it from the bottom of your heart.

Their prayer to make it yet another year
Is based on trust, hard work, and lack of fear.

It takes courage to endure farming's highs and lows.
There are a lot of worrisome sleepless nights, this
the farmer knows.

Without the farmers, our economy would suffer and fall,
So take a moment to praise the farmers and give thanks to them all.

Writer's Block
- B. Begeman

Cascades of thoughts,
images and ideas flowing together in a river of words
only to be dammed by a blank white page,
leaving a stagnant pond in the bottom of a creek
begging for a trickle or at least a drop.

Transparent Life
- Elizabeth Fryer

In billows I lay, white
Life
where sunshine clings like dust,
at Midnight, drowning on a crowded bus,
which sings songs of smoke and rust. Beats to you,
bare fists on a cedar chest, to keep from Thinking,
of Living, of Breathing.
Of turning tunes for eternity.
And morning comes to throw its stones
in bare blue canyons bearing bones
in light, in the presence of you,
love becomes a dance of the rhythm and blues.
Migrants say you hear freedom songs
lapping loudly like waterfalls.
Still, I'm dry and you lay warm, weightless, riding
on some toasting storm,
steel raincoats cover souls of ours. Honest boots
protect our ears, as everyone tumbles
into depths of those whose Tapestry appears.

ⅅRIVEN ONWARD

- Judith Miller Mapes

I remember the tales my
Grandfather told to me
of those many fears
along the trail of tears.

Across the mighty river
our tribe was driven
to the western border
to live by white-man's order.

The snow was deep and
the winds were cold.
Tears were shed by
the young and old.

Though sick and hungry,
they were driven on,
over the mountains
to a world beyond.

No graves were dug,
no prayers were said,
no time for rest,
for it was onward,
onward to the west.

Through Eyes of Love

- Paula Taylor Youngberg

Once I looked into her eyes
In the face of wear and tear

Past the deepness of her eyes
Through the clear, far-reaching stare

Beyond laughter touched with tears
To the warm inner glow

To the strength that few can know
To an angel hiding there

In the tiny person fair
Past toil, past care

Peace was waiting there

One Sunflower

- D. S. Stanley

The seeds face the dirt
Deformed by awkward weight
A jay picks out three
When sunset comes
No one can save me
Yellow is simple
Though it couldn't save
Van Gogh

ODE TO THE WOLF
- Deborah Jacobs

Brave and selfless warrior,
Mammalia Carnivora Canidae Lupus *Canis lupus*,
All praise for the standard you have set
By recognizing that the price
Of liberty must at times
Entail the dispassionate suppression
Of one's own agony,
Which must then be
Masochistically embraced
Through the gnawing off
Of one's own precious limb,
Really a small concession, to secure for oneself
Freedom from the entanglement
Of a predator's devising.
Would that others who believe themselves
More clever than you
Might discover themselves half so sagacious!

SEVEN DEER
- Barbara M. Dickinson

Do you remember the night we saw seven deer?
Granite-grounded, they stood in golden beams
as if frozen transfixed in time.

Breathing man scent and machine fume all turned as one.
Wet brown wide orbs glass-glared umbrage, not fear;
snow-flash blazes blurred as stone leaped free.

Mirror! Mirror!
- Matilde Buch Najovits

On my wall there hangs a mirror,
And exactly opposite
Sits a slightly stooped old lady
Peering wildly into it!

Never! Never! How can it be?
Folks are trying to say–That's Me!
Never! Never! How can it be?
That little old, old, lady–Me?

What about my inner being?
What about my zest for life?
What about the songs I'm singing?
What about the poems I write?

That mirror's face goes to the wall!
That simply can't be me–At All!
I'll turn my heart strings inside out
For all the world to screen,
And show me as I Really Am–
A beautiful, gorgeous–Seventeen!

Untitled
- Carol Schoonmaker

Spring chasing the snow
Into the woods. From the cold
Depths streams bubble forth.

SEASONS

- Cheryl L. Bruce Marcuri

I dance and sing in springtime,
Playing games and dreaming of romance,
Wanting my summer NOW, before life passes me by.

I dance to silent music in summer, now fast,
Now slow, a heady rhythm that confuses and
Enthralls me, wanting everything I see and feel.

I waltz in autumn, stately and gracefully, knowing
The span of time that rules me, and
Remembering the frenetic beat I once knew.

I sit in winter, feeling the cold of forever in
My bones, longing for the rhythms of then,
Knowing that I still dance and sing in my soul.

COBWEBS

- Shelagh Mayson

You hung all Summer,
on hedges, trees, and fences.
Nobody saw the intricate beauty
woven by the energetic spider.
Autumn mists came and, like magic,
jeweled you—
into necklaces of shimmering Pearls.

View from a Bourgeois Bus
- Irene Schuckert

Single file, like ants,
they line up to be "saved" for
one warm night.
Mostly they have black, leathered
faces, grayed with hunger and sallow
in the garish yellow light of a
granite city, trembling
for a cheap grape fix.
A corrugated Jack-in-the-box
shuffles in his ten cent Goodwill shoes
and falls into place as
last-comer.
L. A.'s Main Street swallows up
its dirty laundry through the
mission doors, one time more.
A block away at Temple, the
granite city's Courthouse dispenses
justice,
but there isn't any here.

Together
- Vincenne A. Waxwood

Nature reaches each-to-each:
tree to land
sea to sand;
And I, my dear,
Reach for your hand.

SILENCE

- Barbara J. McKissick

The cat lies on the ironing board;
Only her tail moves now and then.
The tree beyond my window barely breathes.
An ant crawls lazily across the kitchen counter,
Perhaps lost, or abandoned, so seldom are they alone.
The chlorine blue water of the pool sits undisturbed,
Except for a dragonfly that dips and soars
In a summertime ballet.
The sky is washed with yellow cream and still.
Air hot as steam crowds the placid room.
My baby sleeps and I watch so closely
To see the tiny chest rise and fall.
The silence makes a roar within my breast.

CRAYONS

- Jane Anne Romanski

An accident! I swear—it could have happened to anyone.
By mistake I left them out in the sun.
The next day I searched and found them outside,
All melted and waxy and ruined. I cried.
Green blended with purple, orange mixed in with red.
I couldn't believe it, my Crayolas were dead.
I ran to my mom with tears in my eyes,
But before I could speak she gave me a surprise.
A new box of crayons, isn't this neat?
Eight bright and shiny colors. All for me.

The Innocent Mimic
- John Mackenzie

Oddly Mom has spilled some sugar
As she quickly cleared the table
Oddly Dad seems irritated
Oddly both somewhat unstable

So the honest, trusting child
Pure and simple, four years old
With a sculpture in his mind
At the table sits alone

Then some magic in his hands
A King of Hearts becomes a blade
He works with innocence and love
The sugar pile his lump of clay

Now the infant, scared and crying
Off sequestered for his crime
Sits and sadly contemplates
His simple well-proportioned lines

Existence
- Mary H. Gentile

Cycles begin
While others end.
Like Ezekiel's wheel within a wheel,
Whirl, whine, break, and bend,
The perpetual pilgrimage to transcend.

Snow

- Laura Schumacher

Outside, the bitter, cold wind swayed the leafless tree branches,
the grass brown, the sky grey
where it had once been cheerful,
full of life.

Then out of the murky sky
fell
one snowflake
drifting on the cool winter breeze.

Then another.

Before long the land was white,
the delicate white snowflakes swirling around,
each of them dancing to its own tune

until it met with the ground,
and just became
one
in a million.

The Wedding Day

- Cheryl Jones

In a field of wild flowers
Stood a stately unicorn
With coat pure white, a golden mane,
And diamonds in his horn.

I asked him why he stood there,
And with a twinkle in his eye,
He turned his great head toward me,
And this was his reply:

Today I saw a handsome prince
With a beauty by his side.
As they drew near I understood
The beauty was his bride.

I said I'd grant them just one wish,
That I could grant no more,
And they should take some time to think
Of what they asked me for.

I'm still surprised by what they said
As they headed on their way.
They didn't need my help it seems,
For today's their Wedding Day.

They said their hearts were filled with love
To last their whole life through,
And with that I had my answer:
They'd make all their dreams come true.

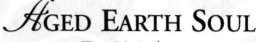GED EARTH SOUL
- Tina M. Anderson

Gathered up from red earth
Shape coaxed into being by the Great Spirit's gentle hand
Life breath given with deepest love and compassion
Gatherer, hunter, nurturer, warrior, and keeper of the earth
Guardian of the earth's creatures
Endured tests of courage, strength, and honor
Endowed with wisdom of the ages
Respects those who came before
Preserves rich heritage and lore of the Earth Soul Tribe
Returns to ashes from the pyre as the soul rises higher
Memories linger on in great detail and song

LEGY
- Geraldine M. Rahilly

When all the world would seem to be
Oblivious of you and me,
We walked together hand in hand
Along the quiet sea-washed sand.
Those days were ours to keep and share.
Those days when you were always there
Have fled away.
So rest beneath the enfolding earth,
Beneath the stone that tells your birth.
While you lie cradled in the land,
I walk alone. I seek your hand.

How to Lure Old Men From Their Chimney Corners

- Lyn Stafford

Mama's calling.
I know she is . . .
But I keep quiet,
Belly-down in the grass,
Running soft green waves through my hands,
Taking sweetness in my nose.

While up ahead are patterns, like furrows,
Where somebody's naked feet
Squashed the blades that grew
In ruts in the mud
And mashed the coolness in their toes.

I'm free.
I can find my way
To the finest meadow . . .
Can break the canes and drink their juices.

"Life," I tell it, "keep away."
My hands are full of grass.
Don't make it so hard to let it go
When I've stopped to play and taste it,
And Mama calls from down the road.

THOSE DARNED SOCKS—
OR UNDARNED SOCKS

- Dan Titus

Folks will agree, if they really know me,
That I'm an easy-going bloke,
And that not many things are a bother to me,
That I like a good tale or a joke.
But there's one blamed thing that bugs me to tears,
That really stirs up my gout,
And that is to find a hole in my sock
With my big toe stickin' out!

I don't mind, if I must, to see nurses and docs
For an X-ray or physical exam;
I am perfectly able to lie on the table
While they probe my guts with their hands.
But it curdles my tea to look down and see,
In full view of that medical crowd,
A big gapping hole in the tip of my sock,
With my big toe stickin' out!

My Lord and creator up yonder in Heaven,
You know I don't ask you for much;
I don't ask you for mansions or luxury cars,
To be healthy and wealthy and such.
What I need from you, Lord, and it's all that I ask,
Is just enough of your clout
To find one pair of socks with no hole in the tip
With my big toe stickin' out!

RAPPERS

- James E. Davis, Jr.

I'm sure this day that I shall die—
just listen, and I'll tell you why—
—those wrappers that you can't get through
will dwindle my days to a few.

That plastic is sealed—oh, so tight.
I tried to open it last night.
My patience, what I had, is gone.
I still can't open it at dawn.

My nerves are shattered, I could cry.
If I don't eat soon, I may die,
and if I do, that bag will be
forever with me, in eternity.

But dare I shout out—as I could—
I'd wake up all the neighborhood.
Unrest and fear I would incite
if I'd resort to dynamite.

I really must calm down and rest,
I've given it my very best.
I'll wait until my wife awakes—
she'll open it in twenty shakes.

THE TREE

- Lita Blevins

One restless night, I had a dream—
So vivid and so real.
About a tree in my back yard
And how it made me feel.

I'd planted it with loving care
And watered it with tears.
Then watched it grow to maturity.
Has it really been 18 years?

One day I turned around to find
It was being broken in two
By a faceless man with a sturdy rope—
There was nothing I could do.

My beautiful tree was gone for good,
I could nurture it no more.
Embracing the stump, I sat on the ground
And wept as never before.

When I awoke from my troubled dream,
My heart ached with grief and pain.
I tried to make some sense of it.
What insight could I gain?

The message then was suddenly clear
When the thought occurred to me,
Remaining in the ground (and in my heart)
Were the roots of my cherished tree.

Where Death Lives

- Greg Price

Grandma,
I went to your grave today
To let you know that
Brown is gone now too.
I remember when we
Brought her to you,
She was such a small pup
You could hold her in the palm of your hand.
You acted like you didn't want her at first.
Back then I didn't understand,
But now I know
As you did then
That if you grew to love her
That someday it would be painful
To watch her die.
Brown was a fighter
Just like you Grandma.
She never gave up.
Towards the end she was
Going up and down stairs and
Doing the best she could.
The day we had to put her to sleep,
She fell over in the kitchen,
Paralyzed by a stroke.
She knew we were there with her
As we kissed her and said
Goodbye.

ℒOVE IS BROWN
- Margo R. Allmaras

Love is Brown, the warm sound of horses
Chinking, shaking their bright silver harness.

Brown smells like leather, a hat and duster,
Bridle and saddle, work boots all dusty.

Brown waves from the field of sun-roasted grain,
Travels to the mill and returns home again.

Brown blazes a trail of gold and red,
Weaves into cloth soft woolen threads.

Brown hands are gentle that brush my hair,
Open a favorite book, then close in prayer.

Brown is love, warmth from the fireplace,
Glowing, dancing dreams upon my face.

ℱOR THE DANCER
- Rebecca Codd

Ballet
The barre is high
She stretches for it, for her dream
A delicate *plié*, a single rose, a standing ovation
She reaches for it, for her dream
The pink lace shines
Fragile

GINGER

- Stella Boyles

Funny and silly 'n' down right giggly
Got to tell ya 'bout Ms. Ginger Swiggley

Nutmeg hair, sapphire eyes, freckles 'n' smiles
Bubble-over laughter for life's long miles

From cut-offs to dresses, sandals to heels
She has more zest than tart lemon peels

Goofy 'n' zany, she's a petite 'lil pip
A dashing lady with get-up-'n'-gone zip

Everywhere at once on her flight through a room
Buzzin' here, there, faster than the sonic boom

A basic hill-billy with a pinch of punk
High on life 'n' full of joy, goodness 'n' spunk

Hobbies and interests are more than a few
Reading and sewing, and her dog "Amy Lu"

Mischievous, ornery, heart of pure gold
Ain't nothing 'bout her cruel, mean, or cold

She's generous, caring, and jelly bean sweet
Being her friend is a Heaven-sent treat

Wishes for a Beautiful Year

- Frances M. Gleichmann

I wish you ——
Bunches of daffodils, spring breezes caressing your hair
Laughter of happy children, friends who care,
Trees like shading umbrellas, raindrops when due,
Blue skies in the morning, sunsets of orange hue,
Meadows filled with clover, wild strawberries and such,
Clouds of yellow butterflies, flowers to touch.
I wish you ——
The tender kiss of a child and warm loving hugs,
Summer moonlight nights with flickering lightning bugs,
Carefree barefoot strolls on the brown sandy beach,
A sail on the bay, a picnic hamper within reach,
A crackling wood fire on a chilly fall eve,
An easy chair, a favorite book you can't leave.
I wish you ——
Winter filled landscapes of dazzling white,
Exciting bobsled rides and a snowball fight,
Food when you're hungry, quiet hours of rest,
Your home filled with happiness and all of life's best,
Days of good health, peace and love,
A year and a lifetime of all of the above.

My Thoughts About Friends

- Pat Alsup

It should be easy
To express one's thoughts,
For it's just how you feel,
But in practice, it's not.
We see something pretty,
Like a cloud on the wind,
Or a tree, or a petal,
Or a smile from a friend,
And we think, that's so special,
I must remember it clear,
So I'll put it in words,
And thus keep it near.
But how do you capture
The phrases to say
What you feel about friends
And their so-special ways?
They accept you daily,
And just as you are.
They laugh when you're silly
And ignore ugly scars.
They help when you're helpless
And cry when you're sad.
Friends stand by your side
Through good times and bad.

THESE TEARS

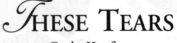

- Carla Kaufman

You said,
"Do not grieve when I am gone.
Go on and live your life.
I could not have been happier
Than I was with you, dear wife.
I loved my job and loved my home.
I've had the very best.
Just remember all the good times
When I am laid to rest."

I listened to your words, my dear,
And swore that I would try.
I'd keep a smile on my face.
No tear would dim my eye.
It was easy enough to promise
When you were with me still.
But now the pain of grieving
Has made me lose my will.

You could not have known
What desolation you left here.
My world is cold and empty now
Since you are gone, my dear.
So when you look from where you are
And hear my sobs, see tears flow free,
Know I cry not for you, my love,
These tears are all for me.

$\mathcal{T}$o: Jesus for Crismus

- Frederick R. Noack

When you wuz jus' a littul boy
Growin' up like me,
What did ya do on Crismus?
Did ya deckerate a tree?

Wuz ther candy canes uv peppamint?
An' men uv gingabred?
An' a turky in the uvven?
An' holly berrys red?

Did ya hang a Crismus stockin'
Aside the fireplace?
An' hear the raindeers comin'?
Get a look at Santa's face?

Did ya wake up in the mornin',
Get up–quick –an' run to see
All the prezzints that wuz waitin'
Unnaneeth the Crismus tree?

Please, dear Jesus, let me know,
'Cuz I rilly wisht I knew,
'Speshly, if on Crismus
Ya got birthday prezzints, too.

MADNESS II

- J. L. Mitchell

Marching round she goes,
round in a circle
her arm upraised in secret salute.
Garbed in black,
her mittens mauve,
she is steadfast in her duty
—to whom or what, that is unknown.
Knees always bent,
her feet lift high,
crisp and steady like the second hand
of an enormous clock.
A clock of her own, always running backward,
she makes her own time
and spends it how she likes,
making peace with the production
she has made
in which she
is its only player.

AUTOBIOGRAPHY

- Alex Norbom

I walk through a tunnel,
dark, damp, lonely;
I strain to see ahead,
dwell on what I have passed,
and stumble on what is beneath me,
falling into the future.

NATURE CALLED

- Marcia Zychal

As the oceans gave way to islands
the islands gave way to man
And the men became ambitious
that's how this all began
As the forests gave way to fields
the fields gave way to towns
And the towns became big cities
that still didn't start any frowns
As the men became hunters
the hunted became extinct
And the animals once abundant
that's how the numbers began to shrink
As the bikes turned into cars
the cars increased pollution
And the pollution destroyed the ozone
that's when man sought a solution
As the powerful became powerless
the powerless are now appalled
And all of this happened because
we didn't hear that NATURE CALLED

ℋis Voice

- John Thompson

I don't remember how he talked.
Now that I think of it,
I can't remember the sound of his voice
Or the words he used.
I can remember how my mother's voice sounded,
How Uncle Randy's rasped,
But when I think of him—there's just a
Warm silence.

I can remember the ferns that grew along the road
And I remember the smell of the hills—
Wild flowers, a distant skunk, horse sweat on the harness.
I remember the slow sweep of a buzzard
High against the sky.
And as the wagon bumped along, we would lean back,
Watching his beautiful dance.
But I can't remember him saying anything.

And finally, I can remember
Unhitching the wagon at the barn,
Pouring oats into the feed box for the horse
While he wiped down the harness with burlap.
But I don't remember him talking.
He was a salesman, talk was his living.
But I have no sound of his voice in my ear.
He is just silent and warm . . . in my memory.

Medieval Dreams

- Christina L. Rice

Of Arthur we're not sure,
Of Lancelot the same,
Gawaine, Garath, and Galahad too,
But they're not the ones to blame.

They were born of myths and legends,
Of fairy tales and lore,
Yet real knights once did roam the lands
Of Europe in the golden years of yore.

Noble they were, valorous and true.
Chivalry then flourished, was nourished, and grew,
While maidens gave their sleeves in tournaments
To those special knights they knew.

Actually, those golden years of yore
Were not exactly golden.
Some knights, not all, stole lands from the poor,
And, of course, there was the plague.

Rough times were they,
Though not every day,
Yet sadly most
Were filled with grey.

So why do so many still dream of those days
When most men were brought up in chivalrous ways?
Because ofttimes the tales told to us in our youth
Are much more dreamy than the stories of truth.

Togetherness

- Adom Anane Firempong

A load borne by many gets lighter.
Happiness shared by many lasts longer.
A bond kept by many gets stronger.
And where many walk in step,
A giant stride is made towards success.

When we share a common dream,
We have a great vision.
And when we apply ourselves to our dreams,
We get closer to the moon
Than anyone would ever dream of alone.

When we put our minds together,
We can solve all mysteries.
And when we join our hands together,
We can move the world.

When we speak with one voice,
Heavens will hear us.
And when we all come together,
There will be nothing between us.

Dandelion Wishes

- Devon V. Grow

Summer
The dandelions appear
Circles of gold
Like miniature suns
Strewn in a green sky
By an unseen hand.

Beautiful
Yellow smiling faces
Pixy delights
The treasures of children
Playing on a summer's day
Under the golden sunshine.

Warming
With rich colors
Signs of the season
Dandelions grow
Mature and fade
As the season passes.

Lightly
Dancing in the wind
Gone to seed
Scattered with the breeze
Blown by a child
With the breath of a wish.

RAVAGES OF TIME

- Terry Cole

She's an old and worn-out gentlewoman,
Her face deeply creased and drawn.
The ravages of time are bold upon her.
Abuse has taken its terrible toll.

Once her future was endless and brilliant.
She sparkled and shone with promise.
Now shriveled, forgotten, and plundered,
About her the air of the unloved.

Yet a hint of majesty still clings to her,
A whisper of what could be.
Could respect and care yet restore her?
Our belittled Mother Earth.

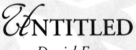UNTITLED

- Daniel Foss

We are going to war,
and we will fight like men,
and we will kill like men,
and some of us will die like men.
But when the war is over,
when the battle is won,
we will look over the dead of our allies
AND enemies,
and we will weep,
WE WILL WEEP LIKE MEN!!!

TRANQUILITY

- Effie Davidson

I walked into the woods today
and stood in awe at what I saw.
I was alone,
yet all around me
life was struggling for existence.
The moss was a carpet of green
covering the ground.
Some looked like little green feathers,
others like pieces of bright green velvet.
The Elkhorn moss ran rampant
over a decayed log that was returning
to the earth that had nourished it in ages past.
The yellow violets standing in clusters
hung their heads as if to hide their pretty faces.
Maidenhair ferns cooled their feet
in the little trickles of water
running down from the mountain.
Giant fir trees stood like guards looking out to sea.
As I stood and gazed at the beauty of nature,
I felt all the hate and bitterness flow out of me.
A feeling of peace and tranquility came over me and
I heard myself whispering,
"Oh, Great Spirit of the Forest,
Make me worthy of Thy creation."

The Path of Wisdom
- Mary Thrasher

That I may not only hear,
But listen;

That I may not only listen,
But remember;

That I may not only remember,
But meditate;

That I may not only meditate,
But apprehend;

That I may not only apprehend,
But practice;

That I may not only practice,
But be.

Idyll
- Gregory Barratt

Day breaks: Eggshell parchment scrolls ashore–
Cleansing, driving dewdrops on before–
Newborn Summer Day.

Thistledown, dandelion, all their ilk–
Flora-fanned feathers of the finest silk–
Lazy Summer Day.

CLOSE YOUR EYES

- Sommer L. Harrison

Close your eyes
Little One . . .
Journey to the Land of Dreams,
Where fairies fly
And dragons roam,
Where your fantasies run free!
Be a maiden,
Pure and true,
Whose beauty is known far and wide.
Knights fight to wear your silken ribbon
To spur their courage on!
Weave a tale in your dreams,
So that even
Great King Arthur would rage with jealousy!
Find the love
Who'd walk the earth for you,
If only to kiss your sweet lips but once.
This is the land where dreams come true,
But only for a time.
So . . .
Close your eyes Little One,
Journey to the Land of Dreams,
Where fairies fly and dragons roam,
Where your fantasies run free!

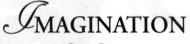IMAGINATION

- Joan Beatty

The night was rainy, overcast, and foul.
In the distance a wolf began to howl.
I quickened my pace and began walking real fast,
As a graveyard I silently began to pass.

Out of the corner of my eye I caught just a glimmer
Of something so macabre I trembled and quivered.
I stood paralyzed, silently watching in fear,
And prayed it wouldn't come near.

This hooded apparition seemed almost to glide,
Coming closer and closer, almost to my side.
My teeth began to chatter, and not from the cold,
And there was an obnoxious odor smelling like mold.

I quickly looked around for someplace to hide,
Before whatever "it" was ate me alive.
My knees were knocking, this wasn't fun.
Then icy cold fingers grabbed me before I could run.

I forced myself to stifle a scream.
Was I having a nightmare? Certainly no dream!
My heart was in my throat and my knees were jelly.
Icicles of fear stabbed at my belly.

Just when I thought I would pass out from fright,
On this dank, dark, and cold Halloween night,
A wee little voice spoke and erased all my fear,
"Grandma, what on Earth are you doin' here?"

Things Not Said

- Elsie Mae Prettyman

Many lines have been written
How words once spoken cannot change.
This time I want to rethink that thought
And its contents rearrange.

The time to say a word flies by,
That time again will not come.
Words left unspoken can't be changed,
An error like that can't be undone.

A time to give a word of thanks,
Or just to utter a word of praise
To make another's road more smooth
Or another one's sad spirits raise,

A time to stand beside a friend,
A time to show someone you care,
If that time you let pass by,
That time again you cannot share.

Time is now a precious thing.
The words you use are tools to build.
Harsh words can hurt, but those not said
Leave voids, too, that can't be filled.

So help me, Lord, my words to choose,
To give those words that are kind and true.
Don't let me leave my words unsaid
That may be used to honor you.

One Moment

- Laima Rozkalns

three hands, not two
both of his
but only one is mine
cinnamon and coconut intertwined

a caress
bewitched
captivated
charmed

his touch is tender, gentle
a brushing glance of a distant wind
bringing smells and tastes from a foreign land
silken tents
hot, dry sand
veiled women
dark, sensuous eyes

one moment . . .

lasting longer than ever could be
engrained into my memory

and so I leave
gone with an impression
and a handshake

FaceWalk

- Nancy Martin

We capture certain seconds in our lifetime,
freeze them forever in frames
that hang upon the walls of our minds,
where we pause during brief walks
through our museum of memories,
refreshing our souls
in silence.

We smile,
we glow,
we renew our faith in being who
and when
and what we are.

Those moments remain corners of happiness
created from the shared community
of family,
of friends,
of love.

And the warmth readily returns
when we gaze once more
at the grace
of good people
who have pictured our lives.

DEARLY BELOVED
- Mary E. Stephens

We are gathered together
Petitioner and respondent
In the sight of God and this company
Each represented by attorneys
To join this man and this woman
Hereafter referred to as "husband" and "wife"
In the bonds of holy matrimony
Reconciliation is impossible
Marriage is a holy estate
Their best interest will be served
Do you take this woman?
Settlement of property rights
Do you take this man?
Custody
I now pronounce you
Child support
Man and wife
With full knowledge and understanding
What God has joined together
Agreement is voluntary
Let no man put asunder
The termination of their marriage

Of Cats and Trees . . .

- Janie Taisler Guidry

Of cats and trees . . .
what can we really know of these?

This attraction of feline to limb . . .
what is the lure that speaks to him?

The leaves call softly with each slight breeze . . .
what are these words that only he sees?

A sudden urge to climb and claw . . .
what need beckoned that only he saw?

Of cats and trees . . .
what can we really know of these?

Perhaps the cat is master of the trees . . .
coming and going as he does please.

Smug, sitting high for all to see . . .
holder of the mystery and also its key.

Content to know that only he . . .
is the keeper of answers not meant for me.

For Better or Worse

- Ellenore Ross

I've lived with this man for nearly forty years.
He's brought me much joy and caused me some tears.
As far as men go, he's near the top of the bunch.
I'll love him forever, but I am not making lunch!

When his work is steady, day after day,
I do my own thing while he is away.
Mop the floor, bake a pie, or paint a wall,
And some days do absolutely nothing at all.

He's a seasonal worker, and as you all know,
That means he's shut down at the first flake of snow.
Home at noon, he thinks "meal," not just a tidbit to munch,
And I think, "Good luck if you're expecting a sit-down lunch."

I get nothing much done, for Heaven's sake,
With my day cut in half by that midday break.
It's company he wants, and ignores my routine,
So for the first few days, I'm feeling quite mean.

When he's home all the time, it takes quite awhile
For me not to flip when he comes in with that smile,
Sheds his coat and hat, takes his boots off his feet,
Checks his watch and declares it's again time to eat.

After weeks of having him around the place,
I learn to relax and enjoy sharing my space.
But I will remember, when it comes to the crunch,
I married for better or worse, but not for lunch!

Mistress March

- Laurie L. Welsh

Mistress March,
Why are you so fickle?
You tease and taunt
With a tender caress
And a gentle tickle.

So capricious,
Just like a spring breeze,
Your sunshine smile turns
To a frosty grimace
With uncanny ease.

An earthy maiden,
You woo with just
A hint of floral scent,
Leaving me to wonder if
Your golden promises were really meant.

Still, your icy fingers
Slowly thaw with ardent desire,
And like the returning robin,
Your winter-weary voice
Joins spring's ecstatic choir.

For as your passion grows
Comes the swelling of your womb.
Your coy promises are finally fulfilled
As the tulips and daffodils bloom.

Fossils of New York
- John Polselli

The chilled ebony highway slips
beneath empty seats, as the steely
guard-railing, defaced with faded graffiti, streaks
like a shadowed subway train outside my heated window.
Solitary bridges, left parted like
starving beaks—darkened buildings, now
deceased, wearing boards for burial clothes, pass
in slow-motion beyond the blur of road lamps.
Night, and the groan of the asphalt seeps
the iron moon deep into black subsequent sleep, while
the city plays out its plaintive role, buried
below the burrows of steamy streets nestled above rooftops.
Speeding cars aspire toward wintry holidays, indifferent
to a woman dressed in rags pushing a rusty shopping cart in
the distance. She too is a relic of the city, who seeks neither
bread nor bone, but the virtue of men
. . . alone, in her heart.

On Picking Cherries
in June
- Patricia J. Brown

Cherries red pierce a blue sky,
Leaf faces framed against the sun.
Eyes-shaded,
I watched your golden head pop above the branches,
Mouth cherry red sweetness.
I laughed,
and hoped I would remember when I am old.

City Streets

- Misty Dobson

People stop to ask the time,
Others sit and sip cheap wine.

Traffic pulses steady but slow
Pedestrians stop, pedestrians go.

Sitting on corners, steps and benches,
Stooping to feed squirrels and finches.

Sporting looks of business and money,
Some look sharp, some look funny.

Walking quickly, jogging cheerily,
Plodding along sad and wearily.

Yawning, chatting, crying, laughing,
Wasting time like it's everlasting.

Rushing and pushing in such a hurry,
Flying by with looks of fury.

Some blend into the wallpaper crowd.
Others stick out big and loud.

Sometimes crazy, sometimes sweet,
Life teams on in the city streets.

o Something

- Jessica Ingles

these are words
blind people can't see them
deaf people can't hear them
foreigners don't understand them
but you do
these words don't say anything
but some do
you could
but these don't
they want to
but they don't
they just do nothing
nothing at all
make no sense
make no rhyme
just hang on this page
like a clock telling time
that is all they do
just sit and stare
they do nothing
like you
sitting there

*V*ISIONS OF THE PAST

- Ethel M. Little

Many a time I looked out the window of our farm house
Only to see the mother cat going to the field to get a mouse.
Then in the spring, when everything comes to life after winter rest
How exciting to see robins gathering things for their nest.
And summer brings the beauty of golden wheat,
As winds blows it back and forth with a beat.
Another sight is the old tire swing,
And how grandchildren loved that homemade thing.
As winter comes with its snow and ice,
Surprises me how the ugliest weed can look nice.
Remember one time we had three kids waiting for the bus?
Now there is only the two of us.
Best of all is we could share it together,
No matter what kind of weather!

$\mathcal{J}$ACKDAW
- Alan Pow

Please can you tell me, Mr. Jackdaw,
Why you chortle, why you caw?
In your mouth you smoke a straw.

You make your bed in a Scarecrow's head.
You rake about in old dustbins
And play *fitba* with two old tins.

You sit upon the stools ungainly
With your head cocked so unmanly.

Why is your waistcoat oh so black,
Or is it the Devil who rides on your back?

You rake up stones for dead men's bones.
You fix me with your glassy stare.

You hobble here, you hobble there,
Then fly away into God's clear air.

You ride upon the winds that blow,
You dark, satanic, beastly crow.

STUDY OF THREE WOMEN

- Mal Morgan

They could be "Les Soeurs,"
But those incandescent faces,
Time havocking the older one

To needle the fairer beauty
Below her breast,
Whilst the portrayal of ugliness
Outshines
And laughter is heard
Ringing in the auditorium
As the nightbell sounds
On jars of ale.
From out the orient
They visit this dark grey capital,
Red buses in similar pose
Across the tarmacadam
Bringing collections of city dwellers
And their worldly counterparts
To gaze and wonder
At three women's dialogue.

A Child's Imagination

- Kristi Leonard-Ros

I see the stars
Resting upon the night's heavy palm,
To shine brightly, then fade away
Before the sun's fingers touch the horizon.
I dream of being a star.

I hear the birds
Chirping gaily to the beautiful day's arrival,
Brushing the morning dew
With their soft, feathery wings.
I wish I were a bird.

I smell the roses,
Faint in the summer air,
Raindrops trickling down their pointed leaves
Like tiny spectrums dangling on a thread.
I wish I were a rose.

I dream of being any of these,
But I am not.
I am only a helpless human child,
With imagination as
My only weapon against life.

The Swing

- Janice K. Jordan

One cold winter's day, I took a walk
Down the alley way, turning into a park.
There I saw it–couldn't stop my stare–
A lone battered swing needing much repair.
It looked so cold and desolate,
As if it'd been years since tiny hands touched it.
It longed for laughter, I could see–
And bright cherub faces so it could free
Itself of the rusty, creaky old chain
That held it so silent–I could feel its pain.
Smiling, I gently touched the tattered seat.
What was that?? The sound of running feet?
Looking around I could see the park was still bare.
It was only the wind, or rustling leaves in the damp air.
In the chill, I stood dreaming another minute or so,
And in emptiness, turning, I started to go . . .
Then with a whisper I thought I heard the swing say,
"Please, for awhile, won't you stay and play??"
I stopped to listen just one last time–
Only hearing the pounding of this heart of mine . . .
But as I left, I thought, "I must!"
So with all my might, gave it one big push!
And as I walked along, I know I heard . . .
The sweet giggling of children and the song of a bird . . .

Virtual (W)rings

- Sri Mukherjee

"We need more memory,"
Marks the hi-tech guy by my side.
Take some of mine or all
And reduce my megabytes,
For I have more than I need,
More than I can ever abide.

What came between us, I wonder.
Was it she or you or I
Or the phone that rings all day,
Wringing our lives, both yours and mine?
What was it all worth it then
Or now as the years rush by?

You hoped it would blow over,
And honestly so did I,
But the net has grown more tangled
While the calls just multiply.
We're caught in this worldwide web,
Like two disks locked in out drives.

I feel against me the hardness,
Not of you but my heart turned tight.
Its density has doubled,
Or maybe just turned high.
Yet the stalker rings all day,
Wringing our lives, both yours and mine. . . .

The Trail

- Sandra C. Obie

An ordinary remote trail
rambled undisturbed
through rough, broken trees,
pushing ever upward
to mysterious regions of the mighty mountain crest.

High above,
feathered tufts of clouds
passed overhead
like silent guardians
of a treasure long hidden.

Cool, patient breezes
chatted briefly
with dancing leaves
and bounced away
as furtively as a kitten in hiding.

Wistful and anxious
like a bubble in a rushing waterfall,
I strayed, an interloper
of discordant harmony
intruding upon this hushed and secret realm.

Verbs

- Patricia J. Carlsen

Maneuver my mind to think all and any of
your wishes.
Evoke my interests, ideals, and dreams.
Escape through me, live within me, exist
for me.
Manipulate language to control me, perplex
me, delight me, anger me, assuage me.
Dilate my mind to accept your thoughts,
adapt your language to my being,
adopt your intricacies.
Ply my senses with rationale.
Educate me to what is within you, around
you, of you.
Tease my reasoning with your motives;
captivate me with expression.
Motivate me to feel, to think, to live!
Extricate me from within the prison of my body.
Heighten me to the vastness of my soul.
Deliver me from my earthly bonds.

ℬLACKEN STONE

- Gerard A. Bell

Not all of them died
Beneath heat-dripping palms
where two worlds should have never met.
Neither are all the victims dead
who were forced to listen—
to the wind and thunder of manmade storms
flooding out the tropic tunes,
the lure of which—
the dead had ears no more to hear,
the living could no longer bear
the strain of listening for.
Hope warbled from the politician's throat
but did not make the flight to 'Nam.
If hope was the soldier's song,
then the ears of those left living grew numb.
For it was the sound of machines
that stood last watch.
As the dead could learn to bury their pride,
the living came home
to accept this war's solitary salute.
So much valor spent—
to earn this mantle of blackened stone
where the dead
became the listed lot, and the living even less renown.

WHY DID DADDY GO?

- Patricia Shroyer

Daddy came to me one night
when I was very small
and told me he must go away
and not come back at all.
He told me that he'd always be
the Daddy I loved so.
If that were true, would someone tell me
why did Daddy go?

The Daddy I had always known
would not have left me so
to wonder what I'd done to him.
He would have let me know.
He would have stayed to dry my tears
until they ceased to flow.
Would someone tell me, if you can,
why did Daddy go?

Many years have passed me by
since Daddy went away.
He's never even called me
or written to explain.
Sometimes I can't remember now,
the memories come so slow.
But the question burns inside my soul,
why did Daddy go?

The Poker Game

- Louise Davis

A long time ago in our little town
Men came in from all around
We had a pool hall they enjoyed
It seemed that it filled a void

There was a room in the back
Where poker was played, that's a fact
The men would play day and night
When wives appeared, it was a fight

One night when there was a game on
An irate wife was there at dawn
She had a gun in her hand
Intent on doing damage and

She shot the window out, it's true
The men did scatter into the blue
Her husband beat her home, it seems
I think he had to change his jeans

The men who play now watch their back
If they hear a noise, they will pack
Their chips and money, away they go
Staying at home and laying low

GE

- Sherrie Nyland

When I turned ten, I wanted to be thirteen.
When I was thirteen, I couldn't wait to be sixteen.
When I turned sixteen, I wanted to be twenty-one.
When I turned twenty-one, I did not want to be thirty.
When I turned forty, I tried to be thirty.
When I turned sixty, I would have settled for fifty.
Now that I am seventy-four,
I just don't care as much anymore.
It took me all this time to realize
how grateful I am just to be alive.

NTERACTION

- Janet Silverman

I interact with the two young men,
the rug shampooers,
and hear myself sounding like my mother.
She's gone now, over a year.
Taken with her is the complete love she gave
to her beloved firstborn,
ME.

Later on, we lived close together, for 20 years.
I saw her interact with people of all ages
who all loved her.
Everyone loved Malka.
She's gone now, over a year.
I'm the senior citizen.
Mom is gone and there's no one between me and
THE END.

$\mathscr{L}$ORDS OF CREATION
- *Philip Cook*

The lords of creation, yes, that's what we are,
Intelligence greater than any by far.
(Unless you know better on some distant star?)

We split and fuse atoms without too much heed
To the endgame for Earth of either great deed.
(We had to respond to our fear and our greed.)

A problem must yield to a clever solution,
In spite of an increase in global pollution.
(We trust someone out there will grant absolution.)

No others before us can claim our distinction,
For thousands of species we've sent to extinction.

Our knowledge we use like a madman frenetic.
We engineer life forms by methods genetic.
(We prefer things to be a little synthetic.)

How will we explain to a far generation
Why Earth is now destined for obliteration?
(But Man after all was a sad aberration.)

The lords of creation, we've been to the moon;
Watch out you poor planets, we'll start on you soon.
('Less you get here first in your silver rockoon!)

STARLINGS

- L. M. Jones

The air vibrates with noise as the Hell's Angels of the bird world arrive.
Black feathered, they gang together whilst regular garden birds
shy away, avoiding the chapter of visitors.
Stud-like their jackets, as with quick maneuvering they parade,
occasional glints as the plumage is caught by the sun.
Alert, the brash leader gathers the clan, and with territorial
rights renewed, the pack organizes, restless to go.
As one they fill the sky, suddenly vanishing, the silence hangs heavy.
Peace returns, and then a Robin begins to sing.

THE RUINED POEM

- Nan Baker

He tried to write a poem
about the loneliness of loss,
of sleeping in a bed too big for one,
with no one to hold onto
when the night drags on and on,
and aching just to see the morning sun.

But then I came along
and held his hand and made him smile
and shared the sea of sheets for just one night,
and filled the empty hours
that had haunted him before,
and ruined the poem that he had tried to write.

*L*OVE WILL NEVER DIE

- Debbie L. Murphy

grief and sorrow come to pass
but love will never die
individual feelings
and words that cannot lie
no-one tells you who to love
there are no rules to play
you build them up as life goes on
learning day by day
they are to you your everything
your special reason why
the life you live, the air you breathe
the joy that makes you cry
for without them, there is no you
no reasons to exist
like a dull and dreary day
a hazy falling mist
so remember all your happy times
and never question why
grief and sorrow come to pass
but love will never die

THE HOUSE WHERE I WAS BORN

- Eileen Eke

This is the house where I was born
Free-range eggs and unkempt lawn
Pigs squealing, what a noise they make
Goat tied up to a very large stake
Allowing no one through the gate
Granddad toiled from dawn to dusk
Whilst Gran made bread and lots of rusks
. . . we were poor!

In winter months icicles would grow
From broken windows covered with snow
But somehow we all survived
And now passing by, in a car I drive
Oh! how times have changed
Nice wide road that was once a lane
Double-glazed windows, sparkling new
Well-kept lawns come into view
No more toiling from morn to night
Farmyard friends disappeared from sight
Our old house that I recall
Has now been named Hastings Hall
You see, we sold it for a 100 quid
But today I wouldn't dare to bid
For 50 years or more have passed
I can't believe they have gone so fast
But if folk ask, "Where were you born"
I smile–recall,
And answer–Hastings Hall

AUGUST IN ENGLAND
- Jackie Holland

Clear blue sky and sunshine
A gorgeous August day
The fields are ripening quickly
Harvest's on the way.

The only clouds are clouds of dust
The ground is desert dry
The land is thirsting
No rain clouds passing by.

Everything looks parched and bare
No grass left on the wicket
Of the village green where dressed in white
The local men play cricket.

UNTITLED
- Timothy Warren

My daughter drove off this evening,
off in the see-your-breath cold night air.
First trip alone, new license in hand,
and those wheels that roll her away
remind me of the wheels that gave me
my breath, my life, my teen freedom.
So why, as more and more circles slowly and silently
lap and surround me,
and the wake rolls over me,
does my heart break, and I feel so old?

PRECIOUS SLEEP

- Robert Hogg

I lie awake, my brain is working.
Tomorrow they will say I'm shirking.
My reason why will set them smirking.
I need some sleep.

Some problems they still need resolving.
Crossword clues, I'm busy solving,
And my thoughts keep on revolving,
Won't let me sleep.

When at last you hear me snoring,
You will not be most adoring.
Keep your curses until morning.
Just let me sleep.

Problems from the night before,
Happily, seem to be no more.
I'm full of pep now, as of yore.
I've had some sleep.

ƐROS

- Mark Ripper

And so one springtime,
We stand among the crowds of Piccadilly
And their cheap affection,
Eros watching the corrupt city
Through white eyes
As the sun drags helplessly away
And the city floods sensitive with evening color,
Advertising endlessly its own death
To the bank-cheques of big business.

Eternally oblivious to the loveless,
Mesmeric among the carcinogenic,
Eros flights his stone arrows
Among the Piccadilly crowds
As we stand in the lilac night,
Hand in hand as the theatres let in
The mystical and the unfaithful
From the storm of sentimental arrows
In the springtime city sky.

THE LADY AT THE BUS STOP

- Joan Wheeler

I waited at the bus stop for the bus to come along.
It was raining–I was fed up–and my hair had all gone wrong.
A lady came and joined me–'twas no one that I knew,
And then she started talking and I found the time just flew.

At first it was the weather and then about her job,
Little stories of her kids and tales about her dog,
And then she started talking of the husband that she had,
And as her tale unfolded, I just knew that he was bad.

She never said his name, she just referred each time to "him,"
And somewhere deep inside I knew her life with him was grim.
I thought about my own life and the man that once was mine,
Who'd walked out of my life, such desolation at the time.

He'd faded from my memory and my life became my own.
I never heard a word from him, his address was unknown.
I met someone and fell in love, so happy now again–
The lady at the bus stop then revealed her husband's name.

She didn't see my face or the expression that was there.
She carried on her story, all the time quite unaware
Of the shock I'd had to hear that name that wasn't new to me,
A name I'd buried long ago within my memory.

I looked away and realized how lucky I had been.
She'd never know just who I was, a stranger she had seen.
Coincidence is what it was, my sympathy was hers–
The lady at the bus stop, with life so full of care.

Meet Me in the Wintergarden

- Thomas E. Grannis

Meet me in the wintergarden
somewhere near the waterfall,
among the lilacs and the roses
where the ivy climbs the garden wall.

Wear your white gown and your veil
covered over with flowers and lace.
I'll have on a white carnation,
waiting for you to take your place.

There be a preacher by my side
just within the chapel door,
waiting there to say the words
that will make us one forevermore.

Meet me in the wintergarden,
and when the chapel bells begin to ring,
walk down the isle towards the altar
as the choir begins to sing.

Meet me in the wintergarden,
and as we kneel and pray,
let me whisper that I love you,
let it be on our wedding day.

SAMANTHA

- V. B. D'Wit

My cat is called Samantha,
She's blacker than the night.
Her eyes are full of secrets
And her heart is full of fight.
And often when I'm resting,
She'll climb up on my chest
And rub her tiny nose on mine
With a quite excessive zest.
Although, sometimes, when in a mood,
She'll give me such a pat–
And stalk off with her tail held high–
"So what do you think of that!"
She knows I am her willing slave
Who always bends the knee.
The lovely compensation is–
She loves no one but me.

SPIRIT DREAMS

- Nora Sprague

They were my secret,
mine alone.
Crazed, ferocious nightmares,
Shadowed, meandering serenities
Hidden from daylight conversings,
Gone since I told you
of them.
I miss the wolves

Summer Storm

- Nancy Davies

Above the tall green trees
The clouds move through sunlight.
The breeze from the river
Carries up high moist air,
And in the sky's blue archway,
The swallow soars and dives
Worshiping the hot sun.

Beneath, the dull stone flags
Trap the warmth underfoot.
The dog pants hard to cool
His big, burning frame.
And in the still, white heatwave,
A woman sighs deep and
Huge, wet raindrops fall fast.

Mississippi Dawn

- Debbie E. Woodruff

Fog rolls lightly over the water at dawn,
slowly enveloping the water creatures in its silent embrace.
All is quiet.

The river is just beginning to come alive.
The sun is rising.
Golden shafts pierce the silvery haze.
Beneath this splendor, the river rolls on—slow . . . silent . . .
and ever-changing.

Capel St. Mary, 1995
- Hugh G. Twose

A droplet of the dew unto the dawn,
And June's sharp sunrise through the hedgerow torn,
Thrusting its oblique rays onto a field of golden corn,

A captured ray upon the dewdrop there,
Whose minorettes of light into the air
Of wondrous hues, a myriad colours told,
On some sweet palette that an angel holds.

And here, lithe pixie dabs his brush with flair
Onto the canvas of the golden air.
All in a trice a picture is begun,
With all the glorious colours of the dew-lit sun.

Window Pain
- Shanna E. Bryant

As the rain falls,
I stare at the drops
on the window pane.

It has to hurt,
to fall from so far
to land so hard.

It's like love.

$\mathcal{A}$ Pilgrim's Quest
- *Anne Voth*

Departed on my own crusade
With quickened steps to distant lands,
Searching for the words withheld, at
Delphi, from the questioning bands.
Honking taxis,
Moaning jets,
Ships with plaintive
Cries at sea,
Fervent cities,
Quaint toy towns,
Vastness rolling
Deep and free.
Returned to ponder myriad answers
In hoary tongues and ancient lays,
Lost the question in the searching
As the babble filled my days.

$\mathcal{U}$ntitled
- *Frederick Blair*

Where do all the mittens go
That little children lose?
Do they go to "mitten heaven?"
Do they go by ones or twos?
Do they look for other hands to hold?
Do they miss their youthful owners?
It's not so bad for those in twos,
But what about the loners?

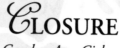CLOSURE

- *Carolyn-Ann Cichon*

I close my eyes to:
wet city streets
sticky personalities
slippery hands
twisted tongues
stone faces and
bleeding souls suffering
deep in agony

Musical tastes
changing constantly with time
confusing lyrics
dance in my head
when I am awake and when I go to bed . . .

Deep in a trance
cold to the touch—I sit in silence
as cold thoughts scream into the night
my souls puts up a vicious fight
for after some time
I simply surrender and
I disappear out of sight . . .

Hiding behind broken fences
hiding behind alluring chemicals
hiding behind distorted faces
I smile without any of my senses . . .

Sweet Saba

- Rosalie Crosby

I must have been just slumbering away
When suddenly I heard my name–and someone say
"Saba–wake up, come with us and play."
There they were, all pitty-patting 'round
And meowing with glee
In a beautiful place called "Kitty Heaven," you see!
Flowers 'n' birds and bumble bees!
Leaving my folks, never to see.
I hurt them, and oh! So much me!
But, they'd be happy to know
I sleep on a cloud and pitty-pat around on the rainbow.
So happy shall I be to stay
In a land of tinklebells and seashells,
And lady-bugs to care for me!
So, purr, purr 'n' meow!

Night Storm

- Colin Frohlick

Last night
I watched the clouds
Assassinate the moon
And thought I heard the cry
Of startled moonbeams
Fleeing from their executioner
And in that moment of perplexity
I saw the heavens weep
And heard the wind
Lament

$\mathcal{T}$HAT OLD TREE

- Rowland Hatfield

As I look into the fire,
I mourn the passing of a friend,
One of significance,
One whose history is ancient,
One that has stood proudly,
Yet witnessed the fall of many.

As I look into the fire,
I see time past,
I see the present
Also passing.
I see times that were important,
I see times that have now lost their importance.

As I look into the fire,
I see a war not yet won.
I see a life being consumed,
However–still giving
A battle that was lost.

THE SIOUX

- Richard Morton

You may see me . . .
I am the deer in flight,
The buffalo thunder,
Or a howling wolf.
Across sweeping plains I run.
Wherever you are, I am there—
I am the Sioux.

You may hear me . . .
I dance with the fire
To celebrate the hunt,
A day fulfilled,
Glorious life
Of untold richness.
I am the Sioux.

You may dream of me . . .
I fly with the shadows
That only eagles will see,
For they are the spirits.

Come with me . . .
To my uncharted lands—
Where we walk with the world,
And we are free.
I am the Sioux.

$\mathscr{L}$ILAC BUSH IN MAINE

- Dorothy M. Osborne

At lawn's edge a stark, spiked bush stoically perseveres,
abides the dark cold assaults and siege of winter.
Brusque, icy winds rip and sever its forked spears.
In this aggression, terror, freezing pain, and numbness,
shivering March winds reactivate a call-to-arms.

Mustering crescent-shaped guard cells to duty—
revives its Spring crusade, restores arrow-tipped buds
to knightly battle skills.

Almost drowning in floods of April rains,
its greening leaves whisper a coded message
about the depth and dumbness
of what it's like to be imprisoned, to face death
in conflict no matter what is right or who is left.

Then protected by a shield of heart-shaped leaves
in sun-warmed May, lunges, en guard,
brave and in true chivalry
presents the *coup de main* to fair June—
luxuriously pointed, purple plumes that anoint
the summer world in lilac perfumes.

OUR LITTLE SECRET

- Melanie M. Sipe

For nine long months there was only
you and me.
We shared so much only you and I could see.

I gave you the hiccups, I got heartburn in
return.
Neither of us really minded, I guess we'll
never learn.

You heard my voice, my heartbeat too
as I quietly talked to you.

I felt you move, all hands and feet,
Our little secret, I thought, how sweet.

You were here with me through good times
and bad.
You're one of the best things I've ever had.

When you left you took my soul.
Sometimes I think I'll never be whole.

Meaning

- Oscar John

On this beautiful early evening I write about not what I understand
But rather what I can not comprehend
I search for an answer that lies within me yet cannot be found
A truth, a resurrection of who I should be
To conquer the dark is life everlasting
To touch your inner Soul and feel it move is to know yourself
Gravity keeps our bodies restricted, but our minds can take us into the
Spiritual world where boundaries do not exist
The imagination is the door to a land that has not perished but is alive
Church bells ring, birds sing songs of passion and honor
Songs with meaningful mourning of lost souls
Rocks dance with one another without ever moving
Leaves float to the ground never, arriving, deep in the ocean fish fly
In the jungle rhinoceros cry
Everything has meaning, even without sound
Birth, blood, bees, skyscrapers, clouds, and trees
Snowflakes melt all around, fires continue to burn bridges to the ground
Everything has meaning
Bushes die, flowers bloom, poets write of everlasting passions
Philosophers argue their views, the media spreads the news
Dirty socks, an empty bench in the park, a pink apron
Everything has meaning, even if we cannot comprehend
Stars reflect shimmering lights in the sky, yet people continue to die
Where have we all gone—everything has meaning . . .

SWING THOUGHTS

- Cheryl K. Hawkins

To feel the cool winds blowing in my face,
drinking hot coffee and swinging to and fro.
Gilbert's watching the birds as they dive low.
I thoroughly enjoy the quietness of this space.

I watched him sleep this morning, as his
eyelashes beat to a rhythm of their own.
The furriness of his body is like a lion's mane.
I cannot yet see what lies in his heart,
Acts real tough, but I know that he's tame.

I am really afraid of letting myself go,
'Cause when I find someone I wasn't to know,
I give freely all that is inside of me.
Then they take my mind, my body and spirit.
Later they don't want near it.

This change that has come over me,
Part wants to hold back, and part wants to be free.
I am not ready to physically love.
I won't be pushed or shoved.
Love shouldn't fit like a glove.

Oh, GOD! How I LOVE YOU!
You changed my old body to new,
Not just this once,
But it's been quite a few.

VANITY TABLE ACCESSORIES
- Nancy Holland-Roehm

Have you ever tried to play with your Mind
only to find a being of a different kind?
For once your typical reactions are noted
and stopped in their tracks
before they are quoted . . .
Reality changes before your eyes
and Life is no longer seen through the guise
of cherished old notions
that served as prime potions
to keep one confined
to old paradigms.

When you taste the new wine so clear and so pure—
distilled from the grapes of a Mind ever sure—
that each new situation demands postulation
befitting its nature and not your own . . .
then mirrors are restored to their rightful place
and no longer are necessary
as part of your face!

And I to My Szeschaun

- Lynne S. Rollins

Mom is standing at the stove frying chicken . . .
a Pall Mall drooping from the corner of her mouth
as I bounce into the kitchen
packing white cartons with Chinese lettering
wearing very big earrings, leather halter covered respectfully
by my college cardigan

dad smiles from behind his newspaper as
Mom covers me in flabby-armed hugs
wincing at my skinniness but saying nothing
I open my dinner as Mom returns to the stove
"What is that?" dad asks curling up his nose
as if peering at a dead body
"Szeschaun beef" I mumble
"oh" dad continues his tirade against the democrats
that began in 1962, flexing his newspaper for emphasis
the TV blips on unnoticed as it has
since my birth

Mother's face brightens as she stirs the mashed potatoes
I read your poem
I didn't understand it, but I'm sure it's very good
Your brother called from Vegas, he'll make $50,000 this year
selling golf clubs, who'd have thought?
Mom serves up the chicken
and I to my Szeschaun

NTITLED

- Richard L. Seiger

Spring flight of soul
Across the evening sun,
Sanctuary in the arms of gods,
The moment of realization in absolute form,
Lost journeys now begun;
Awake upon the dew,
The mist in sorrow and perfect solitude
Brings forth in waves, visions of truth.

Serenity,
The endless divinity,
A symmetric soul across a thousand seas,
Existence so fertile in the womb of time,
The incalculable immanence of infinity.

The omnipotence of veracity
Seems wide and sloping,
Slipping forward, falling downward, swirls,
So complex in simplicity
In the ideals of form,
A haven safe and calm
In the calculus of reason.

Fat

- Jeannette S. Williams

I'm fat,
I know that.
What am I going to do about it?
Don't know.
Ain't done nothing yet.

I think about how fat I am,
And I also think of yams and ham.
Oh, how I wish I could wear a size 5 skirt.
Forget that, I'll have to give up dessert.

I'm starting a new diet.
It worked for others,
So why not try it?

It will last for a little while,
But then I'll get back into my old habits,
My old routine.
Forget the carrots, forget the light cuisine.

Hey, I'm fat.
I know that.
What am I going to do about it?
Don't know.
Ain't done nothing yet.

Machine

- Dennis L. Kuhnel

rampaging collective souls
hushing the sounds of silence
original melancholy spiced with revolution
loss of all that is natural
history's truth in suspicion
roots too thin to weather the fury
origins of humanity replaced by machines
no time to ask questions
being replaced with impermanence
new eager brains corrupted with education
the absolute certified with falsity
wisdom replaced with destiny
the state is mother to everything
whatever happened to individuality
the holy sanctity burning, burning
reality in ruins
absurdity explains everything
bow to the machine

THE RUBBER BAND AND THE WISHBONE

- E. B. Lindak

Poised as a champion slingshot
Tension balanced on each wing
The postal thickness rubber band
And the yellowed, brittle wishbone
Aiming directly forward
Just six feet behind little sister

Small fingers clutching a swirly marble
Take a deep breath
Stretch the arm out
Pull the band back again
Plant its bullet in place
Smoothly let it fly

The band falls slack
Its weight is gone
Quiet satisfaction fills the air around
Until a yelp blurts out ahead

Single Mothers

- Ernest Teague

No one to hold them tightly
or dry the tears they cry.
No one to tell them of their pride
at what it is they try.

No one to share their feelings,
their loves, their memories.
No one left to please them,
no one left for them to please.

They spend their time by themselves,
or with their little ones,
the ones who truly love them—
their daughters and their sons.

Those I speak of should be honored
with a statue of purest gold,
and on a plaque of silver
their stories should be told.

They deserve a special place,
higher than all the others.
These angels that I speak of
are all those special single mothers.

A MUDDY RIVER
- Mark Wyant

Sitting on the grassy bank of the creek,
Feet splashing in the murky stream,
Laughter sings in Spring Air,
Big Bass Splash!

Children chase after kites.
Hopscotch played on
Cracked sidewalks,
Children chant as they jump rope,
Sunsets,
Moonrises . . .

Night breeze brushes our cheeks,
Pleasant soft music
Waltzes from a neighbor's porch
as we embrace,
A gentle goodnight,
Without a word spoken.

Crickets tap dance,
Meadow lanterns flicker in the fields.
Campfire embers spiral upward,
Vanishing in the darkness.

Lonely Black man sings the blues,
Big Bass splashing in Murky Stream
Of a Mysterious Muddy River.

Of Lake Content

- Shannon Schilling

By her shores I spent my days,
Under summer sun.
With golden skin and twinkling eyes,
I remember every one.

Yes, crystal blue, the water hue,
Swimming all the day,
Walking on the stone-lined path,
Flower picking on the way–

And when the rain would come some days
To chase away the sun,
It couldn't stop our games and play.
There was never ending fun.

To this day I smell the breeze
And taste the summer air,
And though I can't return to her,
The memory I share . . .

$\mathcal{M}$ONET'S WATERS

- Isabela Galita-Huin

Cold, dripping materials assembled in ponds
sprinkled with floating lilies
inspiring liquid impressions
with soft displacements
slowly moving the surface
of the humid element that
uncontrolled and disturbing
incontinent and inundating
then suddenly still
reflects the face of the sky
and its cosmic lights
for a blink of unacknowledged peace
mirroring its mathematical features
just before the chemical confusion
troubles the deep grounds
moving the liquid matter
quivering the lotuses
in an uncontrolled laugh
released by the body of this
unnamed phenomenon
and sent in the face of the deaf universe.

Lost sounds from a soft substance
hang unframed on the museum's wall.

Another Love Poem
- Margaret B. Stephenson

I know that you are out there,
Maybe wishing on a star
And dreaming of someone like me–
But I don't know who you are.
How will your sweet voice sound
When you whisper in my ear?
How will your arms feel round me
When you finally hold me near?
What color are your eyes, my love,
What passion takes control?
Do you hurt inside like I do
When some memory takes its hold?
I want to wake beside you
'Neath a canopy of stars–
I know you must be out there,
I just don't know who you are.

Self-Employment and the Single Parent
- Mary McKinley

Anxiety sits
Like my faithful dog
On the threshold of my kitchen,
Watching me cook dinner.
They just sit there, the two of them,
Anxiety and my dog,
Unobtrusive and invasive,
And watch me fry.